LIVING COLLEGE LIFE IN THE FRONT ROW

Jon Vroman

\ 0 /

Cover Design: Nick Mayo

Editing Team: The Vromans (Rick, Patti, and Kirsten)

Author Photo: Marcus Holman

ISBN-13:978-1456580865

ISBN-10:1456580868

This book is dedicated to John Kane: a man who taught me how to live life to the fullest.

I admire, love, and respect you.

CONTENTS

INTRODUCTION

A Selfish Motive

I have a confession to make.

Although I did write this book for you, I'd be lying if I didn't say that I was really curious, and personally wanted to know the answers that are found within this book.

What separates someone who just goes to college to get a degree, and someone who gets the full experience, and then takes their new skills into the after-college world?

I personally believe that if we want to excel in a specific skill in school or life, we should track down those who've already succeeded, and do what they do. More often than not, repeating successful behavior leads to more success. I don't think we need a world of copycats. I'm all for uniqueness and taking the road less traveled. However, when it comes to learning from others, I don't dispute the power of standing on the shoulders of giants. My mentor Tony Robbins says success leaves clues, and my experience of life says he's right.

So, for this book, I interviewed hundreds of students to learn the secrets of success from those who've "been there and done that."

No other book I'm aware of has approached the sharing of stories and strategies like you'll find here.

Mark It Up

Please, please, please…write in this book! Scribble notes, fold the corners of pages, and rip the sides to mark the stuff you really like.

1

When I read books, it's a totally interactive experience. This isn't the library, so treat it like a real learning tool and make it your own.

Also, when you learn something new, or maybe you're reminded of something you already know, put it into practice immediately. Your chance of retaining information after you use it goes up by tenfold, so take action.

Go ahead, try it now, and make a note below. Sketch something. Just get into the habit of what my friend Jon Berghoff says, "Always be taking or making notes."

CHAPTER 1
A FRONT ROW EXPERIENCE

It was the summer of 2005 and one of the greatest musicians to ever walk the face of the earth, Mr. Jason Mraz, was performing a live concert in the city of brotherly love, Philadelphia, Pennsylvania.

My girlfriend and I arrived at the concert early. We pushed our way through the heavy crowds and navigated to our seats. Sure enough, we were in the nosebleed section, the very last row!

It was June 14, my birthday, and I'd been looking forward to this night for weeks.

I remember the place being packed with fans. It was a cool venue, an awesome crowd, and just before we got there, we had a great dinner in the city.

The show was minutes from getting kicked off. I heard some girls who were sitting near the front row scream out, "We love you, Jason!"

The crowd was anxious and ready to rock. When the concert started, the fans immediately began singing and clapping as if they'd heard the song a thousand times—which they probably had!

One thing is for sure, Jason Mraz has a boatload of loyal fans.

As I looked down to the stage, I saw the very front row seats, and I thought to myself, "It would be awesome to have those tickets; row A, row numero uno, the best seats in the house!"

I don't know about you, but I had never sat in the front row at any concert. (I remember searching for U2 tickets once; the front row seats were $15,000 each! Ouch!)

So as I'm hanging there in the balcony, jamming out to the music, squinting to see the stage that felt like it was miles away, something hit me like a tons of bricks.

I thought to myself, "Even though everyone is hearing the same music, it is a totally different experience for the people in front row."

It's like those of us in the back are mere spectators, while those in the front are real participants.

Sure, I was into the music; I was bobbing my head and singing (totally off key I'm sure)...but the people in the front row were really part of the action.

For anyone reading this who has been in the front row, you already know how cool it is, but for those who have not, it's often described as though you are "part of the event" versus being a witness to it.

There is a tangible energy as the music vibrates through your body, or at a sporting event when you can actually see the intensity on the faces of the athletes or when you're at the theater, clearly hearing every word spoken by the actors.

So while I was at the Jason Mraz show having this sort of revelation moment, I said to myself, "This has been my problem my entire life; I've just been taking whatever seat I'm given. I'm settling. I'm living life "in the back row," and to be honest, I'm sick and tired of it!

It was true. Until my mid-twenties, I was in many ways an observer of life but not an active participant.

I thought, "So if I want to be up there, in the front, how do I get those seats?"

Some people would say, "Man...those people are just lucky!"

Sure, luck may play some role in it, but I thought, "I'll bet the people who have those tickets are proactive and focused on getting them. Maybe they have connections, or maybe they were first in line to buy them, or maybe they won them by calling a radio station, or perhaps they just walked up to the front and took an open seat."

Any way you slice it, they made a decision to get in the front row, and they did something about it. They created their own reality. And my guess is that they make decisions and take action in other areas of their life also, not just when it comes to getting great seats at concerts.

Back to my story...later that night, after the concert was over, I found myself standing in the parking lot talking with my girlfriend, and I said to her with passion in my voice, **"I'm sick and tired of my mediocre life. From this point forward, things are going to be different. I'm done being the guy in the back. I want to live like I'm in the front row of a concert, all day, every day, and it's going to start now!"**

It was one of those "enough is enough" moments. You know, that kind of moment when you're fed up with mediocrity, or you're just not willing to stand for the lack of results in your life anymore.

So on June 14, 2005 (my birthday, in more ways than one), in a parking lot in Philadelphia, Pennsylvania, I decided to live life in the front row.

In the months following the concert, certain questions started flooding my brain:

- Why had I been playing it safe in the metaphorical back row of my life?

- What was I afraid of?

- What if I tried my best and failed?

- Could it be success that I actually feared the most? Sticking with the concert theme, what if I got the front row tickets, and other people judged me or were jealous of my seats?

- What was stopping me from really stepping up and living life to the fullest?

- If I did live life in the front row, how would that change things?

- Ten years from today, will I look back on this year and be proud of how I lived it?

Asking myself these questions changed my life forever.

Do You REALLY Want It?

For many of us, if we don't want change in our lives badly enough, we simply won't do anything about it, and nothing will change.

Often times, the pain of what we're getting, or not getting, has to be strong enough for us to take action. If we make change an absolute MUST, then we're more likely to succeed.

For example, you might relate this concept to a time when your apartment was so messy that you said, "This is just flat out unacceptable; I can't stand to live another day in this mess—it's just got to be cleaned!"

Perhaps when it comes to money, you've said, "My credit card debt is totally out of control. I'm cutting up my cards."

Maybe it's with relationships when you've said, "I've had enough of his/her negativity, this is over—I'm serious this time."

Let me ask you…what things in your life are you putting up with that you simply need to say—ENOUGH! I'm going to do something about this once and for all!

Are you willing to stop living life in the back row today and choose to take a front row seat in life?

The world's greatest mentors, coaches, teachers, leaders, classes, or strategies won't change your current life situation if YOU don't REALLY want to.

People have the power to change, but some are just choosing to be lazy, and that's why they won't fulfill their dreams. There are lots of people out there who just want to blame others for the way things are.

Things do not change, we change.
–Henry David Thoreau

7

If someone is committed to holding onto their problems, they'll get to keep them.

We've all heard the old saying, "You can lead a horse to water, but you can't make 'em drink." I like to jokingly say, "You can lead a person to a concert, but you can't make 'em sit in the front row!"

If you're ready to step up and really go after your dreams, then I've got to tell you something before we go on.

When you choose to live life in the front row, people will often react in two different ways.

#1: There will be people who choose to support you: When you're standing up front at a concert and rocking out, I mean having a good ol' time, there are always those people who get inspired by your energy, and they will jump up and join you. By choosing to live life in the front row, you will inspire people, no doubt. Great leaders have the courage to be the one and only person to rise out of his or her seat and spark the standing ovation when everyone else is sitting down.

VIDEO RESOURCE: Check out the video called "Sasquatch music festival 2009—Guy starts dance party" and watch this ONE cool dude spark a huge dance party during a concert.

Now here comes a warning—when you're trying to live your best life, you'll often run into a second kind of person...

#2: The people who will be threatened by you: There is always going to be someone who will get annoyed at the fact that you have better seats than they do, or perhaps they feel that you're blocking their view. Maybe it's simply the fact that because you're having fun reminds them that they are not. Whenever you succeed in life, there will be people who are threatened by it, and they'll try to tear you down. You must be strong. Don't let them affect you.

The real question is, "Are you truly committed to living fully despite the negative people around (behind) you?"

Getting Perspective

Being a great leader means at times being a great follower.

While I love to rock out in the front row, sitting in the back row can also allow a unique perspective.

The back row can teach us how to appreciate the opportunity of being up front.

It can allow us to see the entire crowd and watch their behavior.

If you get tickets in the back, appreciate what you have. I don't believe in ripping up your tickets and declaring, "This is crap. I only sit in the front row!"

Although I'm always in pursuit of a front row experience, I can also learn to appreciate whatever seat I'm given in life.

We all will, at times, find ourselves in moments of life that are less than ideal, and we can either complain about them or we can learn something from them. We all have the ability to make the most of what we're given.

Be the Change

Before we go on, I want to take a minute to congratulate you for picking up this book, and best of all, GETTING STARTED reading it.

I don't even have to know you personally to know something important about you. I know that it takes a certain type of person to not just talk about improving his or her life, but actually do something about it.

Sadly, only about 30% of the people who get this book will start reading it, 10% will get to this point and quit, and only 3% will finish it.

Anyone who knows me personally will tell you that I have a true passion for personal growth. Over the past ten years (I'm thirty-five as I write this) I've invested big bucks (over $85,000) in online classes and courses, personal coaches, and educational seminars; almost anything I can get my hands on that would help me grow and expand. I've read hundreds of books on leadership, time management, engagement, relationships, communication, health, learning strategies, psychology, and business success.

I'm an addict and proud to admit it. I'm a personal growth junkie. I have a healthy addiction to learning the quickest, most efficient, and most down right fun approaches to being extremely successful in life.

I have an insatiable appetite for learning cool things that will make my life more exciting, fulfilling and ultimately, make a bigger difference in the lives of others. I believe that this is my purpose in life. As cliché as that might sound, it's true.

I'm an avid learner because I strongly believe that...

**If we want to change our "outer world,"
we have to first change our "inner world."**

By inner world, I mean that change begins with us, not something outside of ourselves. Gandhi said, "Be the change you wish to see in the world."

By reading this book, by going to school, by surrounding yourself with great people, by taking time to think and by taking action in your life, you ARE changing the world.

My hope is that what's in this book helps you to create an even bigger impact in the world. Inside this book are the strategies for getting more done during the day, having more fun doing it, landing the job of your dreams, experiencing life to the fullest, being healthier, happier, less stressed, being wealthy beyond your wildest dreams, and being more fulfilled.

I wrote this book to be simple, short, and to the point.

It's fast moving, and the goal is to give you the cliff notes about college and life success from some of the most successful graduates I could find.

The most important lessons in this book were written by students for students.

I designed it to help you maximize your experience of college life and with the years that follow. It's the dos and don'ts that help you make the most of your life—right now.

T. Harv Eker said, "How we do one thing is how we do anything." If you want to be successful in life, you might as well start practicing it now.

We are what we repeatedly do.
Excellence, then, is not
an act, but a habit.
–Aristotle

We Become Like Our Environment

Some of my closest friends are also my mentors. They are successful in a variety of different ways.

Some are mountain climbers, and other are presidents of big companies. A few are authors, actors, artists and musicians; while others are moms, dads, teachers, non-profit directors, lawyers, store managers, programmers and doctors. You can even throw in a few philanthropists and politicians. All in all, they are people who are making a big impact in the world.

One way to test what type of person you're becoming is to ask yourself, "What type of people am I hanging out with?"

Then ask yourself, "Are my peers helping me become the best I can be?"

I recently heard Jordan Wirsz, a twenty-seven-year old deca-millionaire, say this, "If you hang around five drunks, you will be the sixth, but if you hang around five millionaires, you will be the sixth. It's better to be on your own than to be around the wrong people. If you hang around people who don't support your ultimate vision, you will be pulled in the wrong direction."

This book will help you create a virtual environment of new friends who have succeeded in life and are generously passing along their best ideas to you.

Shortening the Learning Curve

When I decided to write this book, I did what I normally do when starting a project. I sought out the advice of others. I talked to current students and graduates. I asked questions. The answers I got were so good that I decided to share them with you here.

The people I interviewed are the types of people who by all accounts live great lives, have great jobs, and are making a real difference in the world. They are fun, smart, and talented. They are all uniquely different, yet at the same time, have interesting similarities.

I decided that for this book, I'd interview college graduates who have achieved a high level of success. I see successful people as being happy with who they are, what they do, and that they are making the world a better place through it all.

One of my core beliefs is to learn something from everything. In order to get the most out of college, or life in general, it's smart to learn from others who've walked the path before us. Don't get me wrong, I'm all about paving new paths and being original, but as I said before, I also believe strongly in learning from others—that's just smart!

Some of the people I interviewed have been out of school for just one year, while others graduated over forty years ago.

During the interviews, I asked hundreds of people two very important questions.

> **Question #1:** How did you live college life in the front row? *(Translation: what was the best decision you made during school that helped you succeed most in life post-graduation)*

> **Question #2:** Knowing what you know now about life after college, what would you have done differently given you could go back to school and do it all over again?

After conducting all the interviews, I noticed some consistent answers. I started to see patterns appear about how these

13

individuals approached their college experience and what they would have done differently.

The most common traits from the most successful people were these...

1. Successful people understand the value of **CONNECTING** and having a powerful network of good people around them. We become like our environment, so choosing who we build relationships with is the single most important decision we'll ever make in our life.

2. Successful people are experts in **CREATING** their own success. They excel despite any challenge they face. In fact, successful people often thrive in difficult times. They make the most of every situation.

3. Successful people are open to **CHANGING** their approach to things. Even after graduation, they are students for life. They are innovative and open-minded people who know that even after getting the degree, the real learning has only just begun.

4. Successful people are great at **COMMITTING** to their goals. They will persist until they succeed. Failure is not an option. Being persistent and never giving up are the cornerstones of real growth and achievement.

5. Successful people believe in **CONTRIBUTING**. In life, it's not what we get; it's what we give. Talk to anyone who experiences true happiness, and it's based in what they share, give, or contribute to others. Successful people find a way to give back to the world, and often they are rewarded, both financially and spiritually, for their contributions.

Okay...let's dig in a bit further to each of these points...

CHAPTER 2
CONNECTIONS ARE CRUCIAL

What's the key to real success?

Relationships.

What's the key to real happiness?

Relationships.

What's the key to making a difference in the world?

Relationships.

Nothing in your life will be more important than who you choose to surround yourself with.

Does this excite or frighten you?

A college advisor once shared with me the saying, "Tell me who your friends are, and I'll tell you who you are."

Environment is everything. Strong statement I know, but it's true.

If you connect to a powerful source of energy, you'll get charged, but if you plug into something (or someone) who takes energy from you, you'll end up drained.

The best relationships are those that produce extraordinary levels of synergy.

Check out what these two graduates had to say about making powerful connections while in school...

15

Ryan Franklin
St. Louis University
Class of 2008, Degree in Entrepreneurship

If I could go back in time, and relive my college experience, I would build better relationships with ALL my professors.

Unfortunately, I built very few relationships with professors in college. It was no surprise that those few professors, with whom I did have relationships with, offered extra help, tips, and even project extensions! Cultivating relationships with teachers is one of the smartest things a student can do. Teachers will always go the extra mile for a student who takes time to connect with them. With every teacher, be sure to start the semester by introducing yourself, discussing your extracurricular conflicts ahead of time, and sharing any goals you have for their class.

Brad Weimert
University of Michigan
Class of 2006, Degree in Marketing

If I could go back to college and do it all over again, I would have spent more time and energy nurturing relationships.

Outside of school, it's necessary to make a concerted effort if we want to find new opportunities and meet new people. College could have been a great opportunity to build relationships with a wide variety of people whose lives ultimately took them in very unique, exciting directions. If I were to do it again, I would have respected, enjoyed, and cherished the variety of people available to learn from in college. It would have created great friends and experiences, then and also for the future.

I could write for hours on the subject and power of connecting, but the main point is that one of the keys to maximizing your college experience, and every experience in your life for that matter, is about maximizing your connections (relationships and network).

Investing in relationships is like investing money: there's a compounding effect that takes place over time.

One strategy to strengthening relationships is to look for people who already have great friends and ask, What are they doing right? Do they remember people's names? Are they good listeners? Do they give out compliments regularly? Do they recognize people's birthdays? Do they focus on asking "How can I give to others?" more than they ask "What can I get from others?"

Finish the following sentence with at least ten different answers: I will start building better relationships today by...

1. _____

2. _____

3. _____

4. _____

5. _____

6. _____

7. _____

8. _____

9. _____

10. _____

Jon Vroman

What I Learned from Dave Matthews

In 1997, I saw Dave Matthews play a private acoustic concert at Sweet Briar College. I learned something extremely valuable that would have a profound impact on how I viewed making new connections. Here's the story…

It was a perfect day. The weather was great. I was excited about the show. As I was walking to my friend's dorm room, the halls were totally empty. Almost every student at the school was already sitting on the lawn waiting for the concert. As I strolled down the quiet hallway, there was just one guy walking toward me. He looked like he was in his mid to late twenties, had short brown hair, and was carrying a guitar case with stickers plastered all over it.

I thought to myself, "Look at this guy, trying to look cool in case he meets Dave Matthews. He probably put all those stickers on the case today!"

After I walked past him (judging him), it hit me like a ton of bricks: "Holy $#@*! That WAS Dave Matthews! And it was in that moment that I learned an extremely valuable life lesson, which I'll never forget.

The lesson was not to judge others! **From now on, I would treat everyone like they're a rock star, because they just might be one!**

And to be honest, regardless of whether the people you meet really are rock stars, if you treat them like they are, how would that improve the quality of your relationships?

Remember that often times other people are reflections of ourselves. Call it cheesy, but it's true that when you smile at the world, the world smiles back.

18

Be careful about how you treat others, because you never know who you'll run into again years down the road. Call it karma, but the person you judged in school or treated like garbage may end up playing a role in your life ten or twenty years later.

Focus on building bridges during college, not burning them.

The Anticipation Principle

I got a second lesson a few years later. I was at another DMB concert, and my friend John turned to me and said, "We need to make sure we always have tickets to show, or some other cool event planned. We need to have something we're always looking forward to."

I love his philosophy.

Building relationships is often accomplished through sharing experiences with others.

Since my buddy brought up this idea, I've always made it a point to schedule the next event so we can stay connected. Even if it's a year away, we end up talking for months leading up to the event. Between emails, text messages and phone calls, we'll say, "There only thirty more days until _____!"

I call this the *Anticipation Principle.*

During college there are many cool events going on. Make sure to grab your calendar and plan some time for cool events with friends, or perhaps with the goal of making new ones.

Making connections is important, but finding ways to keep them alive and growing is just as important.

19

So, what exciting events are you looking forward to this semester? Perhaps you can volunteer in some way, or do something to support the community. Don't wait for the perfect event to show up; anything is better than nothing, so just schedule something with people you want to grow closer to and make it happen. Even if it's sharing a cup of coffee—get it planned today.

I should mention that it's important to build great relationships and help others when you're strong, so that one day, when you are the one in need of support, you will be taken care of by those around you. If you spend your time giving to and helping others, when you call on them one day, they'll be more than ready to step up to help you.

Two keys to creating amazing connections:

1. **Be persistent:** The more times we take action by meeting new people, we increase our chance for finding amazing people. You won't build a great network in your dorm room, you need to get out and get into the mix. Connect with lots of people, of course you won't click with everyone, and not everyone will be your best friend, but meeting lots of people gives you better odds of creating extraordinary connections. Just persist in talking to more people, more often, and you'll increase your chances of forming great relationships.

2. **Value your connections:** Students who have created large networks of friends usually have more "luck" because they have more options. Cherish your most valuable resource in life—your relationships. They will play a bigger role in your success than most people will ever understand.

Relationships both on campus and those outside of school are extremely valuable. See what Ali shared about the connection she built with her grandparents.

Ali Mann
Queens College
Class of 2006, Degree in Sociology

I lived college life in the front row by...
strengthening my relationship with my grandparents.

I had a unique advantage as a college student. I was fortunate to pass my grandparents house en route to classes every day. This allowed me to stop in and visit with them more often than usual. What I presumed would be quick hellos turned into unforgettable visits that brought genuine happiness to the three of us. They were curious about my academic and personal life and in return, they shared stories of their adolescent years.

Their stories made me appreciate how fortunate I am to grow up in a world filled with freedom, very different from what they experienced growing up. I left their house and headed to class each day feeling smarter and wiser. I felt empowered by their knowledge about the world. I always knew my grandparents were special people, but it wasn't until I spent real quality time with them that I realized how lucky I was to have them in my life.

If I did it all over again, I would...
have made my visits longer.

My Popi has since passed away and I wish I could have spent more time with him. I will never forget the time we spent together and how it turned me into a more knowledgeable, wise, and strong individual.

21

Let's see what Katherine Otway had to say about powerful connections....

Katherine Otway
Georgetown University
Class of 2003, BA Spanish

I lived college life in the front row by...
surrounding myself with extraordinary people.

This gave me three gifts. The first was that it became the driving force behind much of my decision making. When I was faced with a choice, whether it was to study abroad, join an activity, or take an internship, if I would be surrounded by amazing people, I would choose to move forward. The second gift it gave me was deep, fulfilling friendships because I was becoming more conscious about how and with whom I spent my time. My college friends are admirable and purposeful, thoughtful about their lives and their loved ones. The final gift was the gift of attracting mentors into my life. These mentors, who I admire and trust, have helped in various facets of my personal and professional life and I am still in touch with many of them.

If I did it all over again, I would...
slow down and listen more.

Slowing down would have meant taking my time to complete academic assignments for a deeper level of learning beyond achieving a certain grade, spending more time outside the library, and not overloading my academic, social, and extracurricular schedule. By listen more, I mean I would ask more questions, think more about their answers and just be still. Watch who and what is around. Take it all in and let it become a part of me.

Your Friends' Friends

<u>Fun fact:</u> In the book, *Connected; The surprising power of our social networks and how they shape our lives*, Christakis, MD, PhD and Fowler, PhD, share information about the power of our connections to others, and not only our immediate friends, but our friends' friends!

That's right, it's not just your friends, but their friends can have a great impact on your life. The book stated this, "If your <u>friend's friends</u> gained weight, you gained weight. If your <u>friend's friends</u> stopped smoking, you stopped smoking. If your <u>friend's friends</u> became happy, you became happy."

Video Resource: To see a quick video about this concept, check out Ted.com and search for *Nicholas Christakis: The hidden influence of social networks.*

Six Degrees

Dr. Stanley Milgram, a noted social psychologist, was known for his work with the small-world experiment while at Harvard in 1967. Milgram's experiment developed out of a desire to learn more about the probability that two randomly selected people would somehow be connected to one another.

In the experiment, Milgram sent envelopes to 160 random people living in various cities within the United States asking them to forward the package to a friend or acquaintance that they thought would be closer to a designated final individual.

The letter that was sent contained special instructions. Essentially, it said, "If you don't know the individual who is the final target on a personal basis, do not try to contact them directly. Instead, send this package to a friend of yours who is more likely than you to know the target person."

Milgram discovered that the majority of the letters made it to the broker after passing through five or six different people. This experiment is the source of the more popularly known, "six degrees of separation" concept.

This rapidly spreading idea was at the spark for the game called six degrees of Kevin Bacon—ever play?

Interestingly enough, in January 2007, Kevin Bacon started a charitable organization called www.sixdegrees.org, which is fueled by the concept that we're all somehow closely connected. I believe whether it's six, ten, or twenty degrees of separation, we're ultimately more closely connected than we believe.

Summary Points:

- Treat everyone like a rock star because they just might be one

- The people you choose to surround yourself will be your most essential resource

- Remember the *Anticipation Principle* and get the next big event scheduled

CHAPTER 3
YOU ARE A CREATOR

Do you believe that there are just lucky people, or do you believe that people *create* their own luck?

Growing up, my sister said I was the luckiest kid alive, and while I think that we can all experience a little luck here and there, I personally believe that 95 percent of the time successful people are not just lucky, but rather are good at *creating* their own luck.

Luck is typically defined as force outside of a person's control. During your years in college and the years that will follow, there's no doubt that there are many things outside of your control, but the good news is that there are many more things that are within your control.

Throughout this chapter, I'm going to show you how to create your own reality (luck), to help you get more of what you want and less of what you don't want.

Check out this inspiring story from Ryan, a college grad who was proactive and *created* his own reality...

Ryan Franklin
St. Louis University
Class of 2008, BS Entrepreneurship

*I lived college life in the front row by
starting my own organization.*

Although I captained my varsity racquetball team in high school, I attended a college without a team. Instead of joining a recreational league, I started my own team. After recruiting a handful of mostly inexperienced players, we received over $3,000 from student government for tournaments. After three years with a team of "nobodies," most of whom had never played before college, we placed third in the Mid-West Region behind two national qualifiers. That team has continued its success beyond my graduation. In college and in life, do not settle for what is offered, but create your own fun and opportunities.

In the book *The Luck Factor*, Dr. Wiseman writes that lucky people...

- Create, notice, and act upon chance opportunities.

- Use intuition to make successful decisions.

- Expect the best for the future.

- Transform bad luck into good fortune.

I believe that...

- Luck is *created* by the actions you take.

- Luck is found because you're looking for it.

- Luck is given in proportion to the degree you believe in luck.

- Luck is often disguised as something "unlucky."

26

I believe that the challenges we face in our lives *create* opportunities for us. In fact, I jokingly call these *challengtunities.*

Ryan, in the story above was challenged by the fact that he wanted to be a part of something that didn't exist. Instead of complaining about it, he took action and created his own club.

I've known many people who've taken their unfortunate (or fortunate depending on how you see it) situations to *create* something amazing in their lives by using the challenge as a platform for success.

In this story, Beth decides to create a new version of herself:

Beth Honza
Bowling Green State University
Class of 2004, BA Hospitality Management

I lived college life in the front row by...
taking initiative.

I remember the day my parents dropped me off and the fear and uncertainty of the "unknown" that consumed my mind. However, this uncertainty really pushed me to initiate new friendships and truly *create* **myself as a person**. College isn't just about acquiring the skills needed for the real world; it's also about being inspired (and inspiring others) to be the best we can be at whatever it is we chose to pursue.

When we create success in our lives, we do it, as Beth says, by taking initiative. Great students and great leaders in the world are the best at taking action.

Taking Life Head On

My good friend Hal Elrod was hit head on by a drunk driver at 20 years old. When the paramedics arrived at the scene, Hal's heart had stopped beating for six minutes. Hal was brought back to life, and after six days in a coma with too many injuries to list, he made a full recovery. After the accident, he wrote a book called, *Taking Life Head On* and now speaks to college students around the country about his experience. He found the opportunity within the challenge. He values life even more today because of his accident. Hal *created* his own reality, and didn't let the world dictate it for him. Check him out at www.YoPalHal.com

Miles to Go Before I Sleep

Another amazing person, who I met years ago, is Jackie Pflug. Almost thirty years ago, Jackie was on airplane that was hijacked. The story is detailed in her book, *Miles to Go Before I Sleep*. She's truly an incredible woman. Jackie was shot at point blank range in the head and miraculously lived to tell about it. Jackie now travels the county inspiring others to live life fully. She took a terrible situation and used her experience and what she learned from it, to help thousands of people live better lives. Jackie *created* something great out of a very difficult moment in her life. www.JackiePflug.com

Both of these amazing individuals have used their experiences to serve others, to make a difference, and to leave the world a better place. They have inspired me, and countless others. They remind us that we are not victims, and can *create* success from whatever life gives us.

What challenges are you currently facing?

What are the gifts within those challenges?

The Money Magnet

A good friend of mine is a money magnet! He finds money everywhere!

Is he really a money magnet or could it be that he is consciously or unconsciously looking for money because he believes that he will find it?

My belief is that he is a money magnet because he has positive expectations. He's looking for it, and because of that, the money seems to find him.

Expect to Be Successful

Great students create their own luck because it's what they expect.

Make a decision today to create your own incredible college experience regardless of the fact that you, along with everyone else, will likely have his or her own fair share of things that go wrong.

In fact, plan for it. Say to yourself right now, "When things go wrong, I'm going to find the good in them."

It's not what happens to you, but how you respond to it that makes you successful.

In the end, you can choose to see whatever comes your way as an opportunity to learn and grow.

You create your own success or failure in school, and this will be the case in everything you do, for the rest of your life.
Drew, a graduate of Penn State, shares his experience about *creating* his own schedule, so he could maximize his time in

school. While some students sit around and complain about the heavy workload, or having to work while taking classes, Drew took action and created his own reality by aggressively planning so that he was the one in control.

Drew Frank
Penn State University
Class of 2007, BA in Management
and International Business

I lived college life in the front row by...
Learning early on how to effectively use a planner.

Abe Lincoln said "Give me six hours to chop down a tree, I will spend the first four sharpening the axe."

The first week of each semester, or "Syllabus Week," is when most students finally buy their books and try to shake off the cobwebs from being on semester break. I used this time to plan out my entire semester and prepare myself physically and mentally for the months ahead. I spent almost a full day plugging in every class, every exam, every assignment, when to begin studying for exams and when to start working on outlines and rough copies for papers and assignments. I never got behind in my work and never had to cram for an exam; I was always stress free. I was able to really enjoy my college experience and graduate near the top of my class.

CHAPTER 4
WHAT'S CONSTANT IS CHANGE

"We can't become who we are meant to be by remaining who we are," said Oprah Winfrey.

What do you need to *change* about yourself in order to achieve your goals?

What beliefs do you have about life, people, yourself, and the world, that if you *changed*, would propel you with lightening speed forward in life?

Everyone *changes*. Not always for the better, but things always *change*. In fact, you could say that the only thing constant is *change*!

Even if things are great in your life, I'm guessing you want them to be even better. If you want to progress, odds are that you want to, then you'll need to be open to change.

We all have the power to reinvent ourselves at any moment. That past doesn't have to equal the future. This year can be totally different if we want it to be.

Check out Amiee's story about her willingness to change:

Amiee Mueller
Ball State University
Class of 1998, BA Marketing

I lived college life in the front row by….
reinventing myself.

I grew up in a small town, a poor neighborhood, and with an introverted personality. Being the only one in my family to go to college, it felt like the first time I was around people who didn't have a preconceived notion of me based on my background. I took advantage by forcing myself beyond my comfort zone; I introduced myself to classmates, took a variety of courses in subjects I knew nothing about like anthropology, philosophy, and art history, joined campus clubs, and worked a part-time student job.

Keep the Change

Change can come in small doses. Let me explain.

In my first car, I turned the ashtray into a change dish. My rule was to keep anything silver, but pennies took up too much space, and I would just throw them away. I mean come on…it's just a penny, who cares?

Gas stations do! (And my parents….I'll explain why in a sec.)

Gas stations care about pennies because over the course of a year, it's BIG MONEY. From one station to the next, their price per gallon varies by just a few cents.

Even as a high school student with an empty wallet, I would refuse to obsess over gas prices. My parents on the other hand were always on the lookout for the cheapest stuff in town. It would drive me crazy to hear them talk about how one gas station was four cents less than another. I thought, "It's four pennies!" In their fifteen-gallon tank, that's only a sixty-cent difference. It was not even worth mentioning, but seemed to be a "hot topic" around our house. In fact, every gas station we passed, my mom would say, "Oh look, their gas is only $2.89, the other station was $2.91." I would laugh.

Fact: My parents have never been "in debt." I, on the other hand, have been DEEPLY in debt, which is a sad reality I share with many others (especially students!).

So why were my parents debt free and I was swimming in it?

Simple—my parents were treating pennies just like they treat hundred dollar bills. Money is money. Every penny counts. They don't throw out pennies because they see it as waste. Most importantly, they see something small as a part of something larger. My parents epitomize the saying, "How we do one thing is how we do everything." Look closely at people's daily habits compared to their lifelong successes and failures.

One day "it" hit me like a ton of bricks. If I wanted to create real wealth in my life, I needed to pay closer attention to the way in which I handled the small things as they were indications as to how I handled the big things. For me, my problem was my attitude towards money in general. I failed to recognize the importance of treating money with respect. Once I changed my approach to money, my net worth increased tenfold. This change in my life led to another important question, "Where else in my life was I doing this?"

Okay...now this is where you are supposed to ask yourself, "Where am I doing this in my life?"

Just as people find themselves in debt one dollar (or one penny) at a time, they also find themselves overweight with a few extra pounds by eating one combo meal at a time. In bad relationships, it's one argument at a time. For our environment, it's one piece of litter at a time.

People, places, and things change gradually over time. They are often built up or brought down...one tiny piece at a time.

What small *changes* can you make today that will have a big impact for you months or years down the road?

Here are a few suggestions:

- What about investing small amounts of money, or at least starting a change jar? It's amazing how fast you can save a few hundred bucks by throwing loose coins in an old jar.

- How about replacing just one fast food meal per week with some fruit and veggies?

- Maybe it's studying a little bit each night, and not cramming hours before the exam?

- Or perhaps it's trying to meet one new person each day?

When you make small *changes* each day, over the course of time, they make for BIG changes in your life, and the lives of others.

Making It Count

Take this idea and ask yourself, How can I apply the 'one penny' philosophy to *change* and improve the quality of my life?

Moving forward, I challenge you to treat the "small things" in your life with respect. Understand the power that your attitude towards one penny can have on creating extraordinary wealth in your life.

Find the meaning in every little action. Make every moment count. Instead of thinking that this doesn't matter, instead think about what would happen if you did it 1,000 times, and ask yourself, Would it matter then?

> **A penny will hide the biggest star**
> **in the Universe if you hold it close**
> **enough to your eye.**
> **–Samuel Grafton**

Baby Tiger

As I write this, my son, Tiger, is sixteen months old. A few months ago, my wife gave him some all-natural, plain yogurt for the very first time. I'm not talking about the sugary junk, but the real-deal, no flavor, white yogurt.

When he tried his first bite, his face puckered up like he just bit a lemon. He started to gag a little. Call it child abuse, but my wife and I were laughing at how much he disliked it since he was making some very funny faces.

So, why did we keep feeding it to him even though he didn't like it? Simple. It was good for him.

35

VIDEO RESOURCE: Search for "Tiger Eating Yogurt" on YouTube.com and you'll find the video.

Isn't the yogurt similar to things in our life? Sometimes you don't feel like studying, but you do it because it's good for you. In college, and after college, there are always going to be new things (plain yogurt), that are tough to deal with at first, but if we believe they are good for us, we must embrace the *change*.

Whether it's living in a new town, meeting new people, or starting a new job, CHANGE IS INEVITABLE.

Cathleen Woods
Tulane University
Class of 2003, BA in Business Law and English

I lived my college life in the front row by...
learning how to make friends in a totally new environment.

Arriving at Tulane and not knowing anyone was intimidating. Most of my high school friends went to school in state and I would hear about their parties and feel left out. At first, I clung to my old life and settled for hanging out with people who weren't true friends. By second semester, I made a decision to change and live my new life to the fullest. I played club sports and joined a sorority. While I learned a ton from classes, the best experience of college was studying abroad my junior year. Stepping off the plane with no idea where I was going to live, who I would be friends with, or what life would be like for the next six months was challenging and thrilling.

Change Your Approach...
Again...And Again...And Again...

Babies, just like adults, can be unpredictable. As a new father, I need to be flexible and willing to change my approach.

I learned years ago what was called the ULTIMATE SUCCESS FORMULA:

1. Decide what you want
2. Take massive action
3. Review your results
4. *Change* what's not working
5. Try again and again and again until you succeed

What usually happens, or doesn't happen, separates the "could-bes" from the movers and shakers in the world.

Many people make the mistake of trying the same approach over and over again without making any *change*. Doing what doesn't work, doesn't work.

Even subtle changes can make all the difference.

The only prediction I'll make about your future is that it's going to be unpredictable.

Moving forward, remember these three questions:

1. How else can I view this?

2. What other way can I tackle this challenge?

3. What haven't I tried yet?

> **It's not the strongest of the species that survives, nor the most intelligent that survives. It's the one that is the most adaptable to change.**
> **-Darwin**

Every day, we all get the chance to reinvent ourselves. How will you *change* to become version 2.0 of yourself?

Summary Points:

- Look closely at people's daily habits compared to their life long successes and failures.

- If we increase our awareness regarding the small things in our life, big things will change.

- Be persistent and keep changing your approach until you hit your goal.

- People, places, and things are often built up or brought down…one tiny piece at a time.

- Change that's good for you isn't always easy.

Recommended reading: There's an incredible book written by Chip and Dan Heath called, *Switch: How to Change Things When Change is Hard*. The Heath brothers do an incredible job breaking down why some people change and others don't. Check it out. You won't be disappointed.

> **Where we are is a result of who we were, but who we become is a result of who we choose to be.**
> **-Hal Elrod**

CHAPTER 5
MAKING CONSCIOUS COMMITMENTS

Among the many things I learned from my dad was to really commit to your goals...to be persistent. When I asked my father about his college experience, this is what he said:

Rick Vroman
East Stroudsburg University, Class of 1967
BA Natural Sciences, MS Computer Systems Management

I lived college life in the front row by...
playing on my school's soccer team.

In junior high, I got cut from every team I tried out for except the soccer team, which didn't cut anyone. Fast-forward six years and I am a starting member of a NCAA Division I soccer team ranked fifth in the nation. Life in the front row came from my **commitment** to running wind sprints in the dark after everyone had left practice, never wanting to let my teammates down, and believing when the ball was near me on the field it was MY ball.

If I did it all over again, I would...
have studied harder.

Academics were low on my priority list, a pattern I started in junior high and didn't change until graduate school. I didn't appreciate the incredible opportunity I had to gain knowledge from the professors who had dedicated their lives to educating college students. I went through the motions, making average grades that kept me eligible for the soccer team. In my senior year I started to mature and even made the dean's list, much to my parents' amazement. In graduate school, I graduated with a 4.0 GPA. My advice to undergrads is to be **committed** to making the most of the academic opportunity you have been given. It will serve you well for the rest of your life.

Jimmy Buffett in a Tropical Storm

This particular story begins with a group of friends totally committed to having a goooooood time—and most importantly, the belief that nothing could stop us!

At least that's what the four of us had agreed to while in the car traveling to see Jimmy Buffett live in Camden, New Jersey.

The day of the concert, we packed up the grill, the cooler and tasty beverages before heading out for some fun, live music and the kind of laughing that makes Corona shoot out your nose (if you've never been, this is a Buffett concert in a nutshell).

That night, about half way into the show, the skies opened up and it started pouring. It was coming down in buckets! I remember watching the crowd's reaction to the wet gift from above.

The first type of person was dancing in the rain, laughing at the fact that everyone was soaked; they never skipped a beat.

The other group was clearly annoyed that the rain was ruining their picture perfect event. They were wet, worried about their cell phones, and complaining they didn't have an umbrella.

I once saw a shirt that said, "When life gives you lemons, take a shot of tequila." Said in more PC terms, when life gives you rain, dance in it, embrace it, and let it refresh you. Obstacles that you overcome just make for a better story later down the road. Don't avoid the storm; just play in it. Be committed to your goals and never let anything stand in your way.

Life is like a live concert in many ways, so get up, sing, dance, and live it up big!

Brick by Brick

Whenever you fall, pick something up.
-Oswald Avery

VIDEO RESOURCE: When you get a minute, go to youtube.com and search for "Man Stacks Bricks On Head."

As you watch this video, ask yourself this question, "In my life, am I capable of handling more than I think?"

Thomas Edison said, "If we did all the things we are capable of doing, we would truly astound ourselves."

How do we keep sustained motivation? You must believe that if you're fully *committed* to daily excellence, you'll be creating a lifetime of success and fulfillment.

The world's greatest men and women have created their successes one day at a time. Most superstars are not overnight success stories. Great artwork, buildings, communities, books, movies, relationships are built piece by piece, page by page, or brick by brick.

Personal growth comes from a daily, weekly, and monthly focus on becoming, as my friend and New York Times best selling author Matthew Kelly says, "The best version of ourselves."

Believe in Yourself

In reaching our goals in life, it's important to take note of our current belief system and ask, "Is this belief serving me or hurting me?"

41

Think about the guy stacking bricks on his head, I'm sure someone said, "NO WAY you can put twenty-two bricks on your head at one time," but he did. He was committed to finding a way. He believed in what was possible before he could prove it. He had faith in the future.

- Where have you limited yourself?

- How have you let others limit you?

- What do you need to stop believing?

- What do you need to start believing?

- Are you fully committed to your goals?

Breaking Free

In 2005, I told a few people I wanted to start a charity. Some of my friends were very supportive, while most others looked at me and said, "Oh, that's cool," but I really knew they were thinking "sure you are."

Then I told them that to show my *commitment*, I was going to run a double marathon, it was fifty-three consecutive miles, and I'd do it with only sixty weeks of training. I took on this challenge for many reasons, but one of them was to show my deep commitment to starting the charity and to help raise money to kick it off.

People doubted my intentions, questioned my commitment, and tried to warn me of possible dangers. My physical therapist even told me trying to run that far with so little training was impossible.

To make a long story short, I completed the run, and started the Front Row Foundation (www.frontrowfoundation.org) in 2005, which as I write this, has raised over $350,000 and helped hundreds of people in need. My mantra during my training for the marathon was **A day of pain is worth a lifetime of pride.**

During your years in college, there will be painful days, but if you're *committed* to the end result, you will finish. College is a marathon, not a sprint.

The revelation in this experience for me was **ONE STEP AT A TIME!** Today, this has proven to be a valuable approach to life. One book, one conversation, one compliment, one action, one person, one healthy meal, one day, one decision, one letter, one word, one look, one ANYTHING!

For you, it might be one class at a time, one exam at a time, or one semester at a time. Being committed means taking one day at a time and never giving up.

If I had listened to the naysayers around me, my life would be drastically different today. You will likely doubt yourself at times, and others may plant seeds of doubt in your mind (even people who love you). Friends of yours might drop out and give up, and who knows, maybe that's the best decision for them, but we all must make the right choice for ourselves and be committed to our own personal goals, whatever they are.

We often see people, places, and things in their completed forms, but let's not forget....

- Tall buildings started with one brick being put down.

- Gorgeous paintings began with one brush stroke.

- A baseball team that won the World Series began with one hit.

- Degrees are achieved one class at a time.

43

Earl Kelly Jr.
Wharton School of Business
University of Pennsylvania
Class of 1992, BA Economics, Finance Concentration
Summa Cum Laude

I lived life in the front row by...
fully committing to give my best in every class.

I sat near the front and actively participated. Instead of going back to my room (and wasting time) in between classes, I chose to continue working and maximize my time, reading ahead or rewriting my notes, which helped a ton in test preparation. Bottom line—I learned more and achieved better grades because I was more prepared. I had a good idea what professors would test on because of my participation, and professors knew and liked me, which I know helped my grades on subjective areas like essays and papers. These success habits have also helped me achieve more in life, because I have learned to give my best at every opportunity, which is a trait that helps you stand out from people you compete with for jobs, promotions, etc...

If I had to do it all over again I would have...
become more involved in after school activities.

I had plenty of free time at nights because of my work habits, but I wish I had pursued things like acting, intramural sports, debate clubs, etc. This would have given deeper appreciation of the learning available outside of class.

I challenge you to take this oath today:

I, _____, will commit to having more fun, being more productive, learning more and making the most of every day, regardless of the any obstacle I may face in or out of school.

Signature: _____ Date: _____

Don't take one day of your college experience it for granted. Make some memories. Write the story of your life staring now while you're in school and make it an exciting adventure. To me, this means working harder than you've ever worked, but also playing harder than you've ever played.

Love your life; it's yours, so be proud of it, don't waste another second…go on…get out there and create the next cool story that one day you'll be telling your kids about.

Commit to creating extraordinary experiences in life, and don't let anything stand in your way!

Action Steps

1. **Tell Others:** It's amazing, how much more committed we become when others are counting on us. Let's face it, we're all more likely to show up on time for the gym, make it to a study session, or arrive home for a family dinner when someone is waiting for us. When you involve others in your commitments, you find power that comes with having someone else holding you accountable. Today, share with someone you respect and who has your best interest in mind, one commitment you need to make, but are afraid to.

2. **Write it down:** For years, I've heard different people quote this case study in different ways, but here's a quick recap. This particular study was done with the 1979 Harvard MBA program. Students were asked, "Did you write out clear goals for the future and a plan to achieve them?" Three percent of the graduates did. Thirteen percent had goals, but not in writing and 84 percent had none. Ten years later, the class was interviewed again, and the findings were remarkable, or were they? The 13 percent of the class who had goals were earning, about two times as much as the group with no goals. The three percent who had goals and plans were earning about ten times as much as the other 97 percent combined!!!!

3. **Answer these two questions:**

   a. What will I gain?

   When we're clear about the benefits of our commitments, it's much easier to be motivated to hit them. Sometimes we're our own worst enemy. People ask me, "How do I get motivated?" I often reply, "Just make a HUGE list of all the reasons why you MUST follow through on whatever you're *committed* to."

   b. What will I lose?

   Just the opposite of above, if you're crystal clear as to what the dangers, costs, and problems that come along with breaking your commitments, then you might think twice before giving up early. Sometimes, I'm motivated by fear, and I'm not afraid to admit it. When people ask me what moves me to action the most, I say, "It scares me to death to think about waking up one morning, at age sixty-five, and think to myself that I wasted my life." This moves me to action each and every day. I only get one shot at this life, and I'm not going to waste it!

CHAPTER 6
CONTRIBUTIONS TO BEND HISTORY

How do you personally give back?

When you are contributing to helping the lives of others, whether it's for your family, your friends, or your community, how do you feel?

I often hear people say, "If I only had more time or money, I would do more." That's great that they're thinking about giving, but nothing is more powerful than doing something today.

In my twenties, I realized that I was missing the most important key to happiness—contribution. Yeah, I was giving back in small ways. Technically, I suppose I could justify how I was doing some good by giving a little here and there, but what I'm talking about is that feeling you get when you know that you're doing something great for people.

If you were to rate your level of contribution right now, where would you be on a one to ten scale?

1 = not giving anything
10 = giving at the highest level

Giving can be done in so many unique ways. It's is not just pledging $10 to your friend's walk-a-thon, putting a few dollars in the collection plate at church, or dropping a little spare change in a bucket when the Salvation Army volunteer rings the bell. These are great things to do, but your gifts to the world can be so much more.

If you're totally fulfilled by doing what you're currently doing, then by all means, stick with the plan, but my guess is that you're longing for something more, something a bit more connected or meaningful. There are many ways to contribute your talents and gifts.

Cathleen Woods
Tulane University
Class of 2003, BA Business Law and English

If I could go back in time and experience college life all over again, I would find ways to volunteer my time to benefit New Orleans, a city that needs all the love it can get.

I left a part of my heart in New Orleans, and every time I go back to visit, it pumps stronger and with a renewed fullness. I went to school before Katrina, but even then, there was plenty that could have been done to make it a better, stronger, safer city. I wish I had helped then when I had the chance, rather than feeling like I took more than I gave to New Orleans.

Giving can happen in the most unique ways, let me share with a story about a woman who changed my life.

The Super Fantastic Tollbooth Lady

In 1998, I was driving down a highway when I approached a tollbooth just outside the city of Richmond, Virginia, when a smiling woman, probably in her late seventies, leaned over to collect my $2.00, and asked me, "How are you?"

I have a fairly energetic personality, so I respond enthusiastically, "I'm excellent!"

48

Then, the tollbooth lady said something to me that would change my life forever.

She looked directly at me, a stern straight cold face, pointed at me, and said sharply, "NO!"

I was caught off guard. I thought, "What's up with this lady? What the heck just happened?"

Then, she said with a HUGE smile on her face...

"You..........are...........SUPER FANTASTIC!!!!!"

I started laughing out loud! I smiled so hard my face hurt. Then she gave me in return the most authentic, happy, and full of life smile.

As I drove down the road, I couldn't help but wonder if she says this to everyone or just me. Was I such a special person that she felt compelled to tell me that I was super fantastic? Was she really doing this with every car?

I mean seriously, how long was she working in that booth each day? Eight hours maybe. How many times can you possibly tell someone they're SUPER FANTASTIC without losing steam?

For the next few months, I told everyone about the Super Fantastic Toll Booth Lady. I would say, "This woman is amazing. She's going to be famous one day!"

Sure enough, several months later I was watching TV, and caught the tail end of a McDonald's commercial, and just when the golden arches appeared on the screen out jumps the tollbooth lady and she says, "Try it...It's SUPER FANTASTIC!"

So why did this woman change my life?

I was reminded that regardless of our circumstances, we can find unique ways to give. Some people would have asked the question, "What difference can I possibly make collecting money at a toll booth? It's a lame job. It's boring. It's just a paycheck."

She asked a similar question, but with different intent. She asked, "How can I make the biggest difference with the opportunity I'm given?" She found a way to give. What would you have done in the same situation? What are you doing with your current situation? Are you complaining or contributing?

I like to see our contributions with the "ripple effect" perspective. The ripple effect is the philosophy that one small, seemingly insignificant action, can change the world.

This concept was made popular with what many know as the "butterfly effect," which hypothesized that if a butterfly flaps its wings it could create a tornado half way around the world.

What are you doing with what you've been given?

We can't always change the cards we're dealt, but we can learn to play the best hand possible.

I believe that great success while in college, or any part of your life, is about making the most of what you have. Instead of wishing you had different teachers, a better campus, a little more of this, a little less of that, perhaps you can benefit from seeing the opportunity in what you have right now. We always have something to give.

We can learn a lot about giving from college graduate John Israel...

John Israel
Gonzaga University
Class of 2005, Degree in Exercise Science

I lived college life in the front row by...
almost freezing to death on the steps of our Student Center.

It was one of the coldest days of the year. I was a junior at Gonzaga University. Ten of my closest friends created a program during Homelessness Awareness Week where we collected blankets, jackets, mittens, socks...any article of clothing that could be collected. The week would finish with us sleeping on the front steps of our student center ONLY PROTECTED BY WHAT WAS DONATED BY OUR FELLOW STUDENTS. That night came and we had boxes and boxes of donations to keep us warm. The amazing reality was that this particular night happened to be the coldest night for that day in November in our city's history. It was seventeen degrees or something ridiculous like that. Even with all of that clothing and huddling next to each other, we were still freezing. It really gave me a different perspective on the lives of hundreds of homeless people in our city and a desire to help them any way I could.

If I could go back to college and do it all over again, I would have spent more time organizing or participating in events like this.

College is a time to have new experiences that help us grow in our knowledge of the world and our ability **to make a difference**. I've had plenty of experiences in college that I don't remember, and some that I'll never forget. If it were up to me again, I'd choose more of the latter.

51

How many important life lessons do we miss each day because we fall into a routine of stumbling through our tasks, as if we're sleep walking, not taking notice of the incredible opportunities to give that surround us?

Instead of getting frustrated with your life situation, get fascinated. Get curious, not critical about where you are right now. My good friend Hal Elrod says, "You are exactly where you need to be, to learn the thing you need to learn, to become the person you are supposed to become." I'll add to that, "So you can give to the world what you're supposed to give."

The Super Fantastic Toll Booth Lady reminds us that with one simple contribution, even if they're just words, we can make a lasting impression and perhaps even change the direction of somebody's life.

Some students might say, "I'm just a freshman" or "I'm just a small fish in a big pond. My contributions won't really matter." Well, here's what I have to say about that.

Indifference Makes a Difference

I've got news for you: **You cannot not matter.**

Think about that one.

It's impossible. Even if you show up to class, and just sit there, you are making an impact; you are contributing. What you're contributing is the question. Choosing not to do anything is making a choice to do something. Like it or not, you affect others. You're either part of the problem or part of the solution.

At the end of your college career, what will people say about you?

Will they say that you made a difference by showing up each day, actively engaged, contributing, helping, learning, growing, changing, improving, and having fun?

Or will they say that you missed the boat, failed to take advantage and see the opportunities, or that it's a shame that you wasted the talent that was given to you by a higher power? It's your choice. We all make choices that we have to live with. What will yours be?

Ask and answer these questions:

*   Regardless of my current circumstances, how can I give back right now?

    _____

    _____

    _____

*   How can I better use my strengths to contribute to others right now?

    _____

    _____

    _____

Many people, including me, will doubt our abilities at times, but we must remind ourselves, and remind each other, that we all can contribute to the world in unique ways.

The tollbooth lady is a leader, not by her title, but rather by her actions. Don't wait for someone to appoint you king or queen before you start leading. Just take action, or as I like to say, insert yourself.

Ever feel like you're too young? Don't have enough experience? Not enough time to really give back? Well that's a bunch of crap;

you are the perfect age, you have the right amount of experience and you can always make time for things that matter.

The Lemonade Stand

Check out this story of Alexandra Scott, founder of Alex's Lemonade Stand. She was battling cancer, and wanted to raise money for the hospital where she was receiving treatment. In 2004, sadly, Alex passed away at the young age of eight. To date, with the help of others, her foundation has raised over thirty-five million dollars for childhood cancer research! Alex reminds us that at any age we can have a huge impact on the world and help many other people. Check out her website at www.alexslemonade.org.
Whatever you do to contribute, do it now while you're in school, and you'll start making a difference today. Don't just talk about it, go out and make it happen.

I love the quote, "Your actions speak so loudly that I can't hear what you're saying." That about sums it up!

So Let Me Ask You...

• Are you committed to making your college experience SUPER FANTASTIC by giving back to others?

• What can you do today to start contributing, regardless of how small the action might appear to be?

• If you don't get involved and contribute today, looking back on your life ten years from now, will you be regret not doing so?

CHAPTER 7
THE GRADS TELL ALL

Chuck Berghoff
University of Minnesota
Class of 1973, BSEE

I lived college life in the front row by...
gaining career relevant work experience while in school.

As I worked on my BSEE, I found a job as a technician on NASA space flight equipment. It gave me firsthand experience of what it was like to work in engineering. It also provided me a resume with relevant work experience completed by the time I graduated that resulted in two job offers from an exciting startup company... named Intel. In companies that I've been responsible for running we've offered college intern jobs whenever possible and witnessed real career success stories stemming from intern jobs that related directly to student's area of study. Even a non-paying job, if it relates directly to your future career, will have tremendous value to you at graduation time. You'll have a competitive advantage that others won't have.

If I did it all over again, I would...
learn more about communications and people skills.

As I've progressed from engineer to CEO, I've learned how important solid communications and people skills are to advancing my career. Regardless of what your career is, your ultimate success will depend heavily on your ability to understand what motivates others and how to most effectively communicate your ideas to them.

Betsy Crouch
University of Michigan
Class of 2000, BA Economics

I lived college life in the front row by...
participating in athletics.

I definitely maximized the social opportunities in college. I look back on those experiences fondly. However, I am most proud of my athletic experience in college. I was a captain of the University of Michigan Women's Club Soccer team in 1998 and 1999. I was challenged mentally, physically, and emotionally, as I had never been challenged before. Our team qualified for the National tournament for the first time and lost in the Championship game in a shootout. We knew we worked together well and gave our best effort. The next year after I graduated the team won the National Championship, which was the proudest athletic moment of my life.

If I did it all over again, I would...
have asked more questions.

I believe that my experience was perfect as it happened. To current students: question everything. Ask yourself, what do you really want to study? What are you interested in? I always wanted to take an art class in college and I never did because I wanted to stick with what I thought was "practical." You can dream and be practical. Follow your heart. In addition, see how you can help others have fun. There is someone around you who feels left out. Including them could change their life and yours.

Carey Smolensky
Loyola University of Chicago
Class of 1987, BS Biology

I lived college life in the front row by...
taking advantage of all that my school, and life, had to offer!

In college I went for it all! I was Class President, DJ-ed a weekly radio show, became a certified Scuba Diver, represented my college in Israel for the JUF/UJA Annual Campaign, and became the first Mr. United States (male version of the Miss America Pageant). With my title, I traveled for a year making appearances and escorting celebrities like Heather Locklear. To top it off I met the love of my life DJ-ing her father's party. Not bad for a college experience! Did I mention I was studying biology?

If I did it all over again, I would have...
followed my heart instead of my brain.

Throughout college, I lived at home and ran my own DJ business, making extra money doing what I loved, while studying to achieve a degree for what I though I needed in life. Had I followed my passion, I would have taken a different scholastic path, but I have since learned to live life with passion and follow my heart. I love what I do and wake up each day inspired to make a difference in not only my business, but in people's lives. I don't regret my decisions as they made me the man I am today.

Chris Hammond
SUNY Geneseo
Class of 1996, BA Management Science

I lived college life in the front row by...
enjoying myself without spending too much.

Everyone knows college isn't cheap, and that money can be a source of stress for a college student (and a recent grad for that matter). So be practical and look for ways to save money. For example, buy used books whenever possible. Don't just use the bookstore as a source but contact previous students of that class and look online for deals. Don't overspend on meals. Grocery store specials, with coupons in hand, can save hundreds a semester. And you can find many fun activities to do with friends FREE: local parks, movie nights in, board games, etc.

If I did it all over again, I would...
not wait to the last minute.

Want to have more fun when you are doing any of the countless activities that college life offers? Then do your work first. So many times when I was playing a sport or a game or just hanging around with friends I had a pit in my stomach of the impending test I hadn't started studying for or the paper I hadn't started yet...and was due very soon. Getting started with your work earlier will put you in a better mindset for your fun later!

Courtney Trembler
Endicott College
Class of 2003, BFA

I lived college life in the front row by...
being a competitive athlete.

While I was in school, I continued to be a competitive figure skater. I trained five days a week for about two to three hours a day. I absolutely loved it! It was hard to train for skating and meet all my academic expectations as well as work, but I wouldn't have changed one detail about it! My commitment to so many endeavors kept me focused. As a competitive athlete, I was able to keep in great shape and maintain lots of energy. I found that when I had more things to do, I had less time to procrastinate. In being so productive, I inspired my friends and family to be more productive in their personal endeavors. They would always comment that my enthusiasm and energy was an inspiration. With the knowledge of how others perceived me, I felt motivated to maintain that intense energy and passion. The lives that I touched were rewarded, but truly, it was also a blessing in my own life.

If I did it all over again, I would...
have more confidence in myself.

Looking back, I would have opened myself up to greater experiences in college if I had more confidence in myself. Although people would tell me that I was doing great things, and I felt inspired by the positive influences in my life, I didn't always possess the self-esteem to match. What I've learned since then is that confidence comes from within. It comes from belief in what you are doing, belief in where you are going, and belief in yourself that you are going to be able to get there.

Dan Casetta
Santa Clara University
Class of 1992, Degree in Management

I lived college life in the front row by...
focusing on my EDUCATION, not just my grades.

I have always been a good student and avid reader. During my four years at SCU, I tried to get the most well-rounded experience possible. This meant being active in a job that taught me real-world skills, especially during the summer, and exposing myself to learning outside of school as well through business books and seminars. It also meant having an active social life and getting involved in meeting as many different types of people as possible. Finally, I focused on taking mostly classes that I enjoyed, and by focusing on learning, I did not feel pressured to get a certain grade. I graduated with solid grades, but more importantly, I made the most out of those four years and got a well-rounded education.

If I did it all over again, I would have...
been a little more diligent in my work schedule

Being more diligent during the school year would have afforded me the chance to travel during the summer at least once or during breaks. Since college, I have realized there is so much value in visiting other places with different cultures. Had I made travel a part of my educational experience, I would have gotten even more out of college than I already did.

Dave Powders
University of Virginia
Class of 2001, Degrees in Psychology, Economics

I lived life in the front row by...
getting all of my schoolwork done between 9 am and 5 pm.

I did this so that I could do all the fun things college had to offer at night! Before I learned how to effectively manage my time, I would be up studying until 2 am nightly. Once I learned to stay on campus in between classes, to get up earlier so I had more time to study or get work done, to take advantage of gaps in my schedule allowing me to get work done during the day, I had more free time at night!

If I could do it all over again, I would have...
scheduled more morning classes.

Most students, I find, try to schedule their classes as late as possible so they can sleep in. I would've scheduled my classes all to start at 9 am so I'd be finished around noon or 1 pm, and then I could study until 5 pm, and be finished for the day. This way I'd attend class in the morning, study in the afternoon, and then do whatever I wanted to do at night like going to sporting events, parties, or hanging out with friends.

Don Hill
University of Tampa
Class of 2003, Degree in Business Management

I lived college life in the front row by...
joining a fraternity!

A lot of students just think of a fraternity as a social club that involves a lot of partying. However, what made my experience meaningful and memorable was the leadership experience that I got out of it. The fraternity allowed me to learn about organizing ceremonies and managing events. It also provided an opportunity to enhance public speaking skills as a member of the executive board. I also realize now more than ever the importance of the networking opportunities that the fraternity provided. I now have connections with lawyers, doctors, real estate agents, stockbrokers and others all due to my fraternity experience.

If I did it all over again, I would...
build deeper relationships with my teachers

I appreciate my college experience for everything that it offered me, but I could have made more of an effort to learn from my teachers on a deeper level rather than just the typical student teacher experience. Most teachers are teachers because they love knowing that they make a true difference in the lives of young people. By asking more questions about their business experiences and their stories of success, I could have gotten valuable perspectives that could have brought significant benefits to my future.

Favian Valencia
Gonzaga University
Class of 2004, Psychology/Pre-Med
University of Dayton
Class of 2009, JD

I lived college life in the front row by...
taking the scenic route.

College life allows you to find the best possible way to connect with our global community. By taking the "scenic route," I was able to decide what studies I was interested in. Although I initially wanted to go into dentistry, I decided to pursue the study of law because I developed a greater interest in the influence of our legal system upon our society. I would have never discovered this interest had I not partaken in a wide variety of courses and extracurricular activities. Courses like philosophy, biology, and psychology allowed me to enjoy the scenery from different perspectives. Allow yourself the opportunity to be in the front row while taking the scenic route by exposing yourself to diverse experiences and studies.

If I did it all over again, I would...
have developed stronger relationships.

Although academics are part of the college life, you'll always be able to learn any subject by picking up the appropriate book. College allows you the unique opportunity to develop meaningful relationships with amazing people. Some of the most valuable lifelong lessons I learned through the interactions with my classmates and professors. Seek out opportunities to build meaningful relationships.

Jaime Simpson Krapf
Indiana University
Class of 1998, BFA Ballet, BS Psychology

I lived college life in the front row by ...
cutting my hair.

I began my college life as a bunhead; I lived, breathed, and slept ballet. I was super-thin, with the traditional *long* hair. I was aware there was a world outside ballet, but college helped to really expand my horizons. I took classes like religion and environmental studies; I went to parties (gasp!) I had friends from class, from the dorm, from work. Junior year I cut off all of my hair. Ballet was as important to me as always, but it was no longer my identity. I was a girl in college, who was passionate about many things, including ballet. Don't be afraid to incorporate something new into your life; there is much to explore.

If I did it all over again, I would ...
be better about saving emails and addresses.

I did not stay in Indiana after graduation. There were many people who disappeared from my life as we went our separate ways. I lost their information, and they lost mine. Thankfully, and amazingly, social websites have enabled us to reconnect years later. It's important to stay in touch, in whatever way is most convenient for you. College is a significant experience, and the people you share that with are so valuable.

Jamar Cobb-Dennard
Western Michigan University
Class of 2003, BS Sales and Business Marketing, BA Music

I lived college life in the front row by...
making God my priority.

I had a great religious awakening during my freshman year of college. I spent three evenings a week, Saturday mornings, Sunday mornings, and Sunday evenings at church. I loved being in God's presence, and loved allowing Him to lead and guide me through my college experience. While others were partying away at college, I spent time with God and let him show me his power and ability to impact my life every day. This gave me a strong foundation in Christ that will serve me throughout my lifetime!

If I did it all over again, I would have...
spent more time doing fun college stuff.

I have over 700 people in my Facebook, but fewer than ten of them are from college—and my school had over 20,000 in attendance! I wish I had spent more time going to football games, joining clubs and/or a fraternity, and forming a bond with the people who were sharing the unique experience of college. My college focuses of faith, work, and academics have served me well post- college, but I wish I had done more to create a greater number of fun memories at my alma mater.

Jeffrey Paul Bobrick
Sarah Lawrence College
BA Liberal Arts

I lived college life in the front row by...
participating in the programs I wanted to, regardless of rules!

I pursued arts and academics in a way that made sense to me and was fulfilling. There were exemplary study abroad programs and I wanted to participate in two of them: one at Wadham College, Oxford University, the other at the BADA theater conservatory in London. However, students could only leave for one year. I petitioned the Dean and got permission to leave for eighteen months after I aced senior level courses in my sophomore year. I was accepted into both programs; I studied at Oxford with teachers whose books lined the bookstores, and in London with instructors whose names glowed in lights on the theater and film marquees.

If I did it all over again, I would...
pay attention to what I was going to do in life when I graduated!

Unlike many college students, I focused on education for education's sake. I took every class my heart desired—I made films, and played on the tennis team. While this was an incredibly fun and fulfilling experience, I would have liked to find a better balance between having a great experience (which I did) and planning for my future (which I didn't do).

Jennifer Trask
Memorial University of Newfoundland
Class of 2004, Bachelor of Commerce,
Co-operative (Marketing)

I lived college life in the front row by...
participating in international programs!

The best thing I did during my university years was get involved in extracurricular activities, specifically those in leadership roles and international travel. The number one thing I did was go to a 6-week international business program where I was one of eighty-nine interns from thirty-nine countries. That one experience literally changed my life. Meeting, interacting, befriending, and really getting to know people from that many countries, backgrounds and religions was the moment when I realized that I was in love with the world. My appreciation and understanding of the human spirit was inspired and evoked and has created a love affair that continues to impact both my business and personal life decisions. I now have an addiction to travel; international business and I always have a 'host' no matter where I go ☺

If I did it all over again, I would...
Get Involved, Be Involved, Stay Involved!

The biggest and best learning goes on while interacting with people and being challenged. My advice to anyone reading this is to step up, become a leader, and get organized. Be on committees, run for office, and go on exchanges. Travel if you have the chance and go to as many events as your can. Be social, network and make friends. University is not just about books and exams. It's about experiences. So put yourself in as many situations where you experience different people, places, and situations.

Joe Mancini
New Jersey Institute of Technology
Class of 1999, Degree in Civil Engineering

I lived college life in the front row by...
venturing off campus!

When you go to school in Newark, New Jersey venturing off campus is a little more adventurous than it might sound. During my college career, I had the luxury of rooming with a high school friend. By my senior year, I realized how I was using that as a crutch to limit my social interaction. So I ventured off campus and explored the revitalized downtown area of Newark—I discovered great Portuguese restaurants and interesting local bars; I explored the Rutgers campus across the street and found I could take a philosophy course and the credits would transfer. My new adventurous spirit led me to join the lacrosse club team (even though I had never played in my life) and I made some of the best friends and memories of the entire four years.

If I did it all over again, I would...
spend more time thinking about what I wanted to do instead of
what I was supposed to do.

What a bizarre experience it is being asked to pick a major that will lead to a career that will supposedly be your life's work! No wonder so many of us were "undecided"! If I could do it all over, I would take more classes that had nothing to do with my major—I would think about the infinite possibilities that were ahead of me— I would make more friends—I would explore more places and explore more interests, even if it took me an extra year to graduate. College is an amazing opportunity for self-discovery. Get out there and EXPLORE and figure out what you love to do, the answers are rarely in your textbooks.

Josh Mueller
Kalamazoo Valley Community College
Class of 2002, Degree in Business Administration

I lived college life in the front row by...
accepting delayed gratification as a way of life.

I was on my own to pay my bills, my tuition, and I graduated debt free. Social life and grades were also important, so I learned to work a full time job, manage a full class load, and still find time for friends and family. Simply put, I had to work hard to support myself. My busy schedule forced me to learn how to be responsible with finances and time. In turn, I learned the importance of saying "No" to things that may have been entertaining but did not serve my long-term goals.

If I did it all over again I would have...
utilized the knowledge of my professors more.

I always did my work, turned it in, and took my grade. Knowing what I know now, I am certain I would have enjoyed a much richer education had I spent one on one time with my professors. I've learned that professors love when students show interest outside the classroom. Since college I've spent one on one time with many experts in fields that I take interest in, and I'm always amazed at the extreme value I inherit from each conversation I have with the individuals I spend my time with.

J.P. Hamel
Albright College
Class of 1998, BS Biology, BS Math

I lived college life in the front row by...
following a daily schedule.

I found out that living in the dorms at college was like living in a wicked time machine that would send you catapulting hours into the future without warning. My dorm mates became obstacles to me completing schoolwork before 3 am. I decided that I liked the five-hour post-dinner debates and late-night ping-pong too much to miss, so I constructed a regimented study schedule. This allowed me to stay ahead of the game academically, finish my studying *before* dinner and allowed each night of the week to be a guiltless party.

If I could do it over again, I would...
not stress about small bumps in the road.

Whether a bad grade on an exam or a hiccup in my post college plans, I let many situations manifest in my mind to the worst-case scenario. Realizing that it was just a quick snapshot in time and keeping a positive attitude moving forward would have allowed me to enjoy some of those critical points more and perhaps think more clearly in the days following.

Leeanne Lambert
University of Houston Clear Lake
Class of 2006, BA Communications

I lived college life in the front row by...
getting experience in sales.

Look around you...sales are everywhere! It doesn't matter whether your major is biology, history, or golf...sales experience is something you can apply to every part of life. Sales is more than just selling "something." The company I worked for through college, Vector Marketing, taught me things I never learned sitting in a lecture. A few are: effective time management, leadership skills, goal setting, building rapport, the logic behind consumer psychology and behavior, how to run a business, relationship building, how to train and lead a team, and how to live a balanced lifestyle.

If I did it all over again, I would have...
shared the experience!

Looking back, I wish I had shared the experience I got working with Vector Marketing with more of my classmates. I would not be who I am now if it weren't for the experience I received from them. In fact, even after I graduated, I am *still* with the company and *still* loving it! There is an old saying "find something you love to do, and you will never work a day in your life." While you are in college, find a position with a solid company that is challenging and out of your comfort zone. Soak in all you can!

71

Lindsay Musser
Houghton College
Class of 2005, BA Fine Arts, BA Spanish

I lived college life in the front row by...
studying abroad every chance I got.

Mark Twain once said, "Broad, wholesome, charitable views of men and things cannot be acquired by vegetating in one little corner of the earth all one's lifetime."

During my four years of college, I managed to study in London, the Dominican Republic, Germany, Costa Rica, Nicaragua, Guatemala, plus travel two weeks in Europe with seven friends and a backpack. Most semesters abroad do not cost much more than a semester on-campus, there are tons of student discounts and scholarships. Organizations like athletics or student government will work with you. Plan ahead, work hard to earn the extra money, and be creative. Regardless of your major or financial situation, everyone can find a way to get out of his or her "little corner." You'll see things that change the way you view the world forever, and there's no time better than college.

If I did it all over again, I would...
interview more people I admired.

I did interview a few favorite professors, but I should have done that much more. Who do you know who is happy, and who is regretting certain choices? Be intentional. Learn from others' mistakes and victories and use their wisdom to create the fullest life you can.

Mary Hattum
University of Saskatchewan
Class of 2007, BS Agriculture

I lived college life in the front row by...
having fun and getting involved.

Growing up on a farm and then adjusting to the city life proved a tremendous challenge. I had to make the best of my opportunity, and that's exactly what I did! I got involved in ACE (Advancing Canadian Entrepreneurship), campus rec, horticulture club, ballroom and hip-hop dancing, and two study abroad classes as electives. I did my very best, bravely asked for help along the way, and danced as much as I could!

If I did it all over again, I would....
be okay with not knowing where life would take me.

People always ask, "What are you going to be when you grow up?" I know now, it doesn't matter what you do so much as who you become. I am nature's greatest miracle, already perfect as I am, and everything else is a story I tell myself. Every once in a while lift my dream weights, greet everyday with love and make everyday my best day ever! Remember that I am experiencing what I am supposed to, so I can learn what I need to, to become the person I am destined to become.

Matt Dallas
State University of New York at Albany
Class of 2001, BA Psychology

I lived college life in the front row by...
taking risks and stepping out of my comfort zone.

My most memorable and defining moments during my college years all followed choices that scared me. Whether it was in baseball or my career pursuits, I moved forward on faith that the risk was worth it. I learned so much about myself while growing personally. I think as we grow older, we become risk-averse if we haven't learned how to accept challenges and move forward in the face of overwhelming odds when we are young.

If I did it all over again, I would...
believe more in myself as I ventured into areas I was scared of.

Even though all the risks I took didn't turn out perfectly, I learned from them and don't have to regret not taking those steps. However, if I had believed more in myself and how much influence I really had, I probably would've had better outcomes. Often I came to the end of seasons, semesters, and sales campaigns realizing I could've done better if I didn't doubt myself at the onset.

Matt Storm
University of Houston
Class of 2001, BS Business Management

I lived college in the front row by...
playing sports.

Students run into this challenge all the time. Athletes face it even more... it's the time management challenge. This is and always will be one of the most difficult things to master. Sports develop skills to balance the things college life throws at you...parties, fun, sleep, homework, classes, practices, tournaments, more fun, eating (not in that order). When things get tough, it is easy to stress and want to give something up. When I had more things to balance, things would eventually get easier if I learned how to handle them. Someone once said 'if you want something done, give it to the busiest person. They will put it in their schedule.'

If I could do it all over again, I would...
appreciate more.

Looking back at the memories, college was a time that shaped my life the most. At thirty-two, I still have stories with friends that start with "Do you remember in college when we...!" Having fun was important which happened maybe too much. I was rarely living in the moment. I was too busy looking at the big picture. Looking back, I wish I enjoyed more of the process instead of worrying so much. The common truth is 90 percent of our fears never happen anyway. The major worries were really minor. Learn to laugh when the world feels like it's ending. What memories and stories will you have?

Michael Bankus
Penn State University
Class of 1985, BS Economics

I lived college life in the front row by...
being prepared ahead of time.

All of my high school teachers liked to use the line, "When you get into college...." They had me scared that there was going to be an overwhelming amount of material and homework. That summer, before entering college, I enrolled in the Evelyn Wood Reading Dynamics speed-reading course. I drove an hour and a half each way to Philadelphia for six weeks. That first semester I applied all that I learned about reading three times faster while increasing my comprehension. It paid off by enabling me to handle the workload and be more effective. Make sure you do a self-assessment and get the skills you need ahead of time!!

If I had to do it over again, I would...
appreciate the unique experience of college.

College is a time where you can build relationships, learn more about yourself, and, hopefully, not worry too much about producing income. Yes grades, achievements, and resume building are important, but it is those relationships that you will take with you once you leave. Focus on the goal at hand, but don't forget to also build some great friendships for life!

Mike Monroe
Boston College, Carroll School of Management
Class of 2003, BA Operations, Finance

I lived college life in the Front Row by...
being an academic superstar.

I was in the Honors Program, graduated *Summa Cum Laude* with the highest GPA of my major, and almost had enough credits by my senior year where I could graduate twice. By the end of first semester, I had accumulated a 3.98 GPA (got an A- in a one-credit ethics class) and was committed to staying excellent throughout my four years. At graduation I was presented with the *John B Atkinson Award*, a beautiful mahogany clock, and praises from the Dean and my parents.

If I did it all over again, I would...
prioritize my time differently.

I was involved in numerous other organizations and my academic work would often times default to Thursday, Friday, even Saturday nights. I remember many times sitting at my computer and saying "not tonight" to people who came by soliciting my presence to the evening's big party. To all you academics out there: keep saying "not tonight" and people will eventually stop asking. I'll never know what memories I could have made had I spent more time with people instead of pleasing people. My mahogany clock broke years ago and I don't remember my final GPA.

Phil Geertsema
Minnesota State University
Class of 2007, BS Management

I lived college in the front row by...
having a balanced life.

I look back at my college years and smile; I loved college. I took full advantage of the social aspect; I was on the Dean's List a couple of semesters; I spent time with important people in my life; and I was always in great shape. During the point in most people's lives where they gain the "freshman forty," I worked out five days/week, gained muscle and lost fat. I found that if you want to do something bad enough, you will find time to accomplish that activity. "I don't have time" isn't a valid excuse; you have to make the time.

If I did it all over again I would ...
not settle for mediocre grades.

Most people in college, myself included, study only to get good grades, not necessarily to learn. This produces a problem: most students settle with *just getting by*. This creates an attitude of mediocrity that extends beyond college. Life is about getting the most out of every experience, not about *just getting by*. If I could go back, I would have read ahead in textbooks, participated in the class discussions and I would have studied *better*—with an intention of remembering the information beyond the test, I could use it later in my life.

Robert Danbury
University of Colorado at Denver
Class of 2009, BA Geography, Environmental Studies

I lived college life in the front row by...
participating in extracurricular activities.

Although I felt that focusing on school was important, I also never thought it should be the only thing. This way there's more to look forward to than just classes and grades. By participating in activities that were both fun and challenging, it let me use my energy in multiple areas and not feel bogged down by the pressure of just doing one thing. I played soccer, did Karate, had a weekly game night with friends, and a job. This allowed me to pursue personal growth and interests while maintaining a balanced life and going to school.

If I did it all over again, I would have...
taken more out of those classes that I didn't think I needed.

There were a few required classes and electives I took that I felt were a waste of time because they had no application to what I was doing with my degree. I had to take the classes anyway, but it would have been more beneficial for me to go in with a different mindset of "what can I learn" as opposed to "why do I have to do this?" It's surprising how useful that information can be once you get out into the world.

Rhancha Connell
York University
Class of 1991, Honours Degree Political Science

I lived college life in the front row by...
becoming a master at time management.

In high school, teachers stay on top of you and push you. In university, it's a very different story; if you want to succeed, you are going to have to do it on your own. You need to hold yourself accountable because no one else will. I worked with Vector during my University time and they truly helped me to plan and organize my life to achieve all my goals. They encouraged me to use a day planner from Day 1! I stayed on top of all my assignments as well as maximized my social life. Once I received the course outline and deadlines for all assignments and exams, I could schedule the next few months of my life. I went to concerts, never missed Pub Night ☺, sporting events, along with family and friend times were all scheduled in my organizer.

If I did it all over again, I would...
get more involved in activities on campus.

I lived off campus and I think that might have contributed to me not getting more involved. There are so many great organizations on campus and by getting involved with them, it adds to your resume. It exposes you to new people and new ideas. As a student, we don't really think too much of the future and what it means to have an amazing resume after you graduate. Summer job experience definitely helps, especially when you work with Vector, but having other cool stuff on your resume makes you stand out to an employer. Being President of a club or a group on campus shows that you have leadership skills. Employers are looking for this. I know a lot of us say we don't have time to do it all but when you have your life organized and planned out, everything will get done.

80

Sara Beth Sims
Sweet Briar College
Class of 2003, BA Theatre Arts

I lived college life in the front row by...
living up to every responsibility that was expected of me and
more.

As a single mother at the age of nineteen, I found that not only did I have to step up to the plate and take on the responsibility of being a mother, but that I also needed to go beyond that in my college experience so that I could show my little one what kind of a role model I could be. I worked two jobs, took twenty-four credits a semester, double majored, typed papers late into the night, worked on every production our theater had, and still drove to and from daycare every day. I found that the more responsibility I was willing to take on and complete, not only the more organized I had to be, but the more I realized that the best role model I could be....was to be the best that I could be!

If I did it all over again, I would...
take more pictures of all the things I experienced.

I sit and reminisce with friends from college telling stories, and laughing so hard that our faces ache, as we try to fill each other in on the things we no longer remember. The more ways you can keep these memories fresh in your mind, the more you will hold and cherish the experiences and lessons you had. Hold them fast, smile, and click!

81

Scott Butler
George Mason University
Class of 1989, BS Physics

I lived college life in the front row by...
excelling in academics.

I did not take the "straightforward" route to college. I spent two years playing on the beach in Southern California and painting houses for a living. It was an amazing experience. I "sowed my wild oats" and also learned what it took to exist on my own. I decided that I wanted more out of life and that my ticket to new possibilities was a college education. When I got to school, I was able to devote myself to succeeding in college, graduating as quickly as possible, and excelling in the process. I achieved a 3.9 grade point average and was elected the outstanding junior and senior physics student. I completed my schooling in three and a half years.

If I did it all over again, I would...
get more involved in "outside of the classroom" campus life.

I went to a college that had a large commuter population including myself, and I never took advantage of many of the excellent programs that my school had to offer, nor did I forge many lasting relationships with other students in my classes. For many people, college is one of the most exciting times of life. They forge friendships for life, find business contacts that help them succeed beyond college, and are able to have amazing experiences outside of the classroom. If I had it to do all over again, I would take the same passion I had to excel academically and apply that to many other aspects of the college experience.

Stacey Martino
Rutgers College School of Business
Class of 1993, BS Accounting

I lived college life in the front row by...
Making a great decision before going to college!

When I was applying to colleges, the big question was, "What's your major?" Most of my friends picked subjects they found "interesting". That seemed "undirected" to an A type personality like I was back then! So I decided to pick a JOB first and then pick the major that would get me that job. I think I did it backwards, but it ended up working out great for me! I got exactly what I wanted out of the deal: a kick-butt job!

If I did it all over again, I would...
NOT have based my decisions on security, certainty, and
significance!

Like many overachievers my age, I wanted a powerful and high paying career when I graduated college. *Translation:* I wanted the significance of a powerful employer and I wanted a high salary so I could support myself without depending on anyone. Where you choose to spend your days is so vital to your fulfillment and happiness in life. Basing that decision on fear based (although rational) reasons, will only lead to days that leave you looking for more and saying "is this all there is?" If I could do it all over again today, I would spend some time deciding who I wanted to be in the world FIRST and then pursuing my destiny and my dreams on my terms!

83

Sunday Lewandowski
University of Pittsburgh
Class of 1996, BA English Literature

I lived college life in the front row by...
participating in athletics.

Without athletics, college would have been a bore. Being a key part of the Swimming and Diving Team kept me on my toes. My supportive teammates provided me with drive, inspiration, and loyalty. We studied, practiced, and laughed hard. We had each other's best interests at heart. However, as a seven-time NCAA All-American and Olympic Trials finalist, I faced many challenges. The lessons I learned then have helped me immensely in my professional life now. I feel confident knowing that I possess the perseverance it takes to confront any flip, twist, or turn life throws.

If I did it all over again, I would...
not have cut corners.

Little did I know that everything I cheated on would later catch up with me! As an English teacher in Miami, FL, I am required to instruct an ever-changing curriculum and new material somehow always turns out to be a concept or philosophy that I was supposed to have studied years ago. Instead of being a professional, I feel more like a fraud. To heal my lingering guilt, I skip days on the beach and redo what should have already been done. Cutting corners in college has haunted me for years. Is it "Karma"? As aggravating as this may be, I must do it. I love my career. So I spend my days reading Shakespeare and Homer, analyzing theories of Modernization . . . while my friends catch the surf. It's a compromise that could have been avoided.

Tom Skawski II
Augustana College
Class of 1996, BS Pre-Med, Biology

I lived college life in the front row by...
getting involved in anything that sounded interesting.

In my senior year of high school, I got active in a few things. I amplified this concept in my college years by volunteering, attending, joining and engaging in anything my school had to offer that sounded interesting. I worked in the theater, got active in my dorm government (and was later elected into student government), played IM sports, volunteered for service organizations, and enrolled in a social organization that has spawned some lifelong friendships. If I wanted to do it, I did, even if it was out of my comfort zone. Challenge yourself to get interested and get active.

If I could do it all over again, I would have...
not take my education for granted.

Learning isn't just about classes. Inter-personal relationships aren't just between your friends. Learning to interact with teachers and administrators is important. It's also important to learn **how** to interact with these people. I'm extremely grateful that I live in a country where I am free to get educated, but I think many students take this for granted, I was no exception. I had a lot of fun in college, and I didn't flunk out. But, I also could have taken my classes much more seriously and applied myself. And I also could have taken the out-of-classroom lessons to heart.

Zak Kraft
Emory University
Class of 2004, BBA Marketing and Management

I lived college in the front row by...
taking classes that were outside of my comfort zone.

Although I was a business major, I decided to enroll in two history classes and an organic chemistry class designed for non-pre-med majors. Although science and history were not my favorite or strongest subjects in high school, I found that I had a much stronger appreciation for learning during college and thus really enjoyed the classes.

If I did it all over again I would...
study abroad.

I missed an incredible opportunity to see the world, experience different cultures, and make new friends—all while having few responsibilities at home. It was not until after college that I developed the urge to travel and experience the world. I really regret missing out on café con leche in Spain during my college years.

I believe that this day, or any day for that matter, is our chance to turn over a new leaf.

I believe that we are charged with the responsibility of making the most of what we have been given.

Brad, a college graduate from Michigan, does a great job of summarizing what this book is really about.

Brad Weimert
University of Michigan
Class of 2006, BS Marketing

I lived college life in the front row by...
pushing myself and finding out what I personally was capable of.

Throughout my college career, I worked for a direct sales company. Their sales competitions seemed to light a fire inside me to prove what I was capable of. While the financial reward was gratifying and the sales experience was beneficial, it was the beliefs I established throughout my college years that allowed to me excel as a professional. Consciously or sub consciously people judge their capabilities by what they have done in the past. College proved to be an amazing time to establish powerful beliefs. Aligning myself with an opportunity that rewarded me to push myself and expand my beliefs became one of the single most important components of my life.

F O U N D A T I O N

A portion of the royalties from this book will go directly to support the Front Row Foundation.

This charity, which I proudly serve, helps people **"experience life in the front row."** The focus is to help individuals and their families who are braving life-threatening illness to live their lives to the fullest by providing front row seats to concerts, sporting events and live performances of the recipients' choice.

The goal is to create magical moments that positively affect the mind, body, and spirit of each person involved, including our sponsors and event organizers.

The Front Row team is made up of dedicated volunteers who believe that even just one powerful experience can be transformative. For those who are braving critical health challenges, any positive experience, especially those that involve their favorite team or musician, can be a life-changing moment and memory.

The Front Row experience helps individuals to put aside any physical or emotional challenges while they celebrate the beauty and emotional energy of life.

Front Row Foundation was born in a community of close-knit family and friends, many of whom were and currently are college students, who want to make a difference. It is our belief that a group united in passion and common purpose can have tremendous power to "bend history."

Great moments in our lives are remembered forever. Together, those who support the Front Row Foundation will create lasting memories for those in need, one positive, incredible, and life-changing experience at a time.

Someone once asked me, "Jon, why do you put so much effort into front row tickets?"

For anyone reading this who's been in the front row, you already know the answer.

There is a tangible energy. The music vibrating through your body, the intensity in the faces of the athletes, the voices of the actors provide that energy.

Finally, it's not just sitting in the front row at any event; the goal of the organization is to have people sit in the front row to see their favorite sports team, musician, or show, and that is what makes Front Row Foundation so special.

The big vision is that one day, every band, venue, and ticket agency will be sponsoring a front row recipient at every concert, sporting event or live performance...in the world.

There won't be an event taking place, anywhere in the world, without someone sitting there, hands in the air and "living life in the front row."

That may not take place for another hundred years, but one day, it will.

MEET OUR RECIPIENTS

Sophie's Kelly Clarkson Experience

(Sophie in her mother's arms. Kelly on left.)

On October 12, 2007, four-year-old Sophie, who was diagnosed with a brain tumor, met her favorite singer, Kelly Clarkson. Sophie and her family were in attendance for Kelly's outstanding performance at the Borgata Hotel and Casino in Atlantic City, New Jersey…and of course, watched from the front row! The day began when a fifteen-passenger stretched limousine picked up Sophie, her parents, Lauren and Jeff, her two aunts, and grandparents at their home in Southern New Jersey. The forty-five-minute ride to Atlantic City ended at the Rainforest Café where they shared dinner with elephants, gorillas and there was even a thunderstorm, right in the restaurant! Following dinner, they experienced a fun filled night at the concert where they sang their hearts out! Finally, the entire family enjoyed a suite at the Borgata Hotel and Casino. When the night ended, Kelly was huge fan of Sophie….and with that smile, who wouldn't be?

Ethan's Philadelphia Phillies Experience

On Wednesday, April 8, cancer fighter Ethan was treated to an incredible experience. As Ethan's Dad tells the story, "Thanks to the generosity of the charity group Front Row Foundation, we were able to enjoy a Phillies game from behind home plate in the third row!! After our chauffeured limousine ride to Citizens Bank Park, we watched the pre-game World Series Ring Ceremony and cheered the Phillies on as they pulled out one of the most exciting wins in years! Yes, it's true if you think you saw us on TV, you really did. Our seats were in an area that was visible at certain points during the Ring Ceremony and a couple times during the game. Ethan declared the day "Awesome!" and "one of his best ever."

Before they came back with their big rally, he told me, "Dad, even though they are losing, I'm still having fun." Jake was even lucky enough to get a couple game balls tossed to him by guys on the field. Make sure to ask Ethan and Jake to tell you all about the limo ride and game when you see them next. To get the full effect of just how close we really were, visit my Picasa gallery and view the Phillies game file. This magical event was created by advisors of the Front Row Foundation John Kane and Loretta DiCiano and friend of Ethan's family, Dawn Hopkins.

Glenna's Christina Aguilera Experience

(Glenna, in the middle, with her best friends)

Glenna is a strong and passionate twenty-four-year-old who has been diagnosed with Stage IV Melanoma. She has undergone many treatments and has spent countless hours in and out of hospitals, but on March 30, 2007, she was given the opportunity to put all that behind her for an "Front Row" evening with her friends.

It all began when the black stretched limo arrived to pick up Glenna and six of her best friends at 5:45 pm. The group was whisked off to enjoy a fabulous meal in the gorgeous city of Boston. Glenna and her friends reminisced about all the great times they had together as they laughed the evening away. Glenna was beaming. They continued on to the TD Banknorth Garden to enjoy the Christina Aguilera concert from the FRONT ROW! When they arrived, there were back stage passes awaiting them, and the ladies were escorted by Christina's production crew to the side of the stage where they were allowed to enjoy the sights and sounds of the show.

It was a tremendous experience for all involved as Glenna was enthralled by the passion of the performance and the company of her great friends. The night was an experience that none of them will ever forget.

To learn more about the Front Row Foundation and how you might be able to help provide a magical moment for someone special, please email info@frontrowfoundation.org or drop by the website at www.FrontRowFoundation.org

Here are a few ways you can get involved:

- Register for our newsletter at
  www.FrontRowFoundation.org
- Connect with us on our Facebook Fan page at
  www.FrontRowFanPage.com
- Host a fundraiser on or off campus
- Spread the word by talking to your friends

A FRONT ROW PHENOMENON

Almost daily, the foundation receives pictures from our friends "Living Life In The Front Row" to show their support and spread the word about our cause. Whenever you find yourself living life to the fullest, appreciating the moment, and fully engaged in life, then join the club by taking a picture with your hands up pointing to the sky, and send it to info@frontrowfoundation.org. The photograph of the month wins a free Front Row t-shirt.

Here are a few of my favorites.

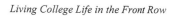

Your Picture Here

THE TEN BACKSTAGE SECRETS EVERY ROCK STAR STUDENT MUST KNOW

Students who live life in the front row tend to do these ten things better than anyone else. How would you rate yourself in each area? What can you do to improve in each area?

1. Put It Out There

I like the thought "begin every day as if it were on purpose." Write down your three most important goals each day on a piece of paper and keep it in your pocket. Ask yourself throughout the day, "Is what I'm doing right now getting me closer or further away from my goals?"

2. Move It or Lose It

Concerts are more fun when you're standing up, singing, and dancing. It's like when you were a kid and your mom would say, "Put down the video game or stop watching TV, get outside, and play." Get your blood pumping, and you'll feel better. Each day, with the amount of studying that you do, or time in classrooms, it's essential to make it a point to do something active: play a sport, go for a jog, or throw a Frisbee on your lunch break. Just get moving.

3. Give It to 'Em Good

I've yet to meet someone who doesn't appreciate a sincere compliment. Sincere being the key word. You can find something nice in every person; sometimes you have to look hard, but trust me it's there. Admire everyone like you would your favorite musician or athlete. Remember from chapter 2 about connecting—treat everyone like rock stars! Compliment them like you're their biggest fan, and soon enough, they'll become yours.

111

4. Don't Read Until It Hurts, Read Until It Feels Good

People are more interesting when they're reading something interesting. Personal growth is like investing. Steadily depositing new information into your brain daily, no matter how small the amount, adds up. Don't just read what you're told to read: read what you want to read.

5. Feed That Body

Just like filling up a car with gas, you've got to fuel your body the right way: drink water instead of an energy drink; eat fruit and vegetables instead of a double death burger. REAL energy is crucial to living a passionate and exciting life...for a long time. When you graduate and get a job making lots of money, don't you want to be around to enjoy it? Someone once told me, "Make easy decisions today, life is tough on you tomorrow, but make tough decisions today, life is easy tomorrow." Eating healthy isn't always easy, but neither is any form of real success. Replace one unhealthy snack today with something more wholesome. Most students overeat, so at your next meal, leave one bite of food on your plate just because you can. You should dictate how much you need to eat, not the person serving you the food. Don't spend your youth building your wealth only to end up one day spending your wealth trying to regain your health. Start now and choose to be healthy from this day forward.

6. Do It Differently

Spice up your day today. Be spontaneous. On your way to class, take a different route. When you click on Pandora.com, choose a new station. Go somewhere new for lunch. We won't become a better version of ourselves by doing what we've always done. What can you do differently today? Break the routine a bit and stretch out of your comfort zone. If something isn't working, don't do more of it! I recently heard, "Doing more of what doesn't work, doesn't work!"

7. Be in the Present

Gandhi once said, "Live as if you were going to die tomorrow and learn as if you will live forever." Treat each day as if it were your last. Tell a friend or family member that you love them. Appreciate every day because you're paying for it with your life. Feeling better about your current life situation is easy to do when it's put into perspective. Whatever challenges you might have, someone else has problems ten times worse. I hear it all the time. People return from a third world country and say, "I'm so grateful that I live in America." Nothing gets you to appreciate things in life that we normally take for granted, like electricity, running water, and freedom.

8. Do the Tough Stuff First

It's natural to gravitate toward the path of least resistance. Usually the project that will make the biggest difference in your life is pushed to the bottom of the list. Build emotional muscle by putting yourself in challenging situations today. Good students will do today what others won't so they can live a life tomorrow that others can't. Instead of waking up and doing something simple just to check items on the list, tackle the toughest projects first and feel great the rest of the day.

9. LOL

Remember to have fun. Life is short. How often do you laugh during the day? Find one clean joke today and tell it five times. Oh, what the heck, make it dirty! Just kidding. In fact, I want to laugh too, so email me your best clean joke today at jon@jonvroman.com.

113

10. Get the Gift

We can't control everything that happens to us, but we can control what meaning we attach to it. When you're faced with adversity, ask yourself "What can I learn from this?" or "What's the gift in this?" There are seeds of greatness in every difficult situation; sometimes you just need to look closely to find them.

YOUR LEADERSHIP BRILLIANCE

My life was changed forever when I was once asked the most incredible question:

> If today were my last day on Earth and I could share
> 500 words of brilliance with the world, what are the
> important things I'd want to pass along to others?

This is the powerful and thought-provoking question that an incredible woman by the name of Gail Goodwin, founder of inspiremetoday.com, asked me during a recent interview.

I personally believe the best questions to ask others are not those you want answers to, but the ones THEY want answers to. This was a question I wanted to know the answer to.

In a moment, I'll share with you what Gail calls "My Brilliance." Perhaps for you it will be simply a quick reminder of things you already know or believe, or maybe it will spark a new feeling, thought, or belief; either way, I hope it enhances your life in some small way. Here was my answer…

If today were my last day on Earth and I could share 500 words of brilliance with the world, the important things I'd want to pass along to others would be...

1. Be a strategic architect for the environment of your life; nothing will impact your future more than the information you consume and people you associate with.

2. Relationships are THE key to happiness; choose your friends carefully.

3. Find peace in forgiveness, both in yourself and others.

4. *Learn to express compassion while holding yourself and others to high standards.*

5. *Ask yourself and others quality questions and listen intently.*

6. *Having extraordinary relationships is more often about becoming the right person than finding the right person.*

7. *Learn how to meet other people's needs without neglecting your own.*

8. *Do not shrink yourself in order to please others: live fully.*

9. *Refuse to get wrapped up in drama and negativity; we see what we seek in others and ourselves.*

10. *Get fascinated, not frustrated; curious, not critical.*

11. *Value the wisdom of others while following your heart.*

12. *Develop a reputation for giving. Do nice things for people anonymously who can't repay you, however, remember that giving to yourself IS essential in giving to others.*

13. *You were born to contribute and share your gifts with the world.*

14. *Be an ambassador and force for all that is good.*

15. *Take care of your body; it takes care of you.*

16. *Laugh and smile so that your face hurts.*

If you liked 1 through 16, you can get the rest of the list, numbers 17 through 38, by downloading the full free copy at www.FrontRowOnCampus.com.

MY CHALLENGE TO YOU

So, now let me ask you, "If today were your last day on earth, and you could share 500 words of brilliance that would be read by others for generations to come, what important things would you want to pass along to them?"

Your thoughts can be about anything you feel is important. They can be about life, leadership, success, giving back, relationships, education, teamwork or anything else you feel would be the most valuable information you can share.

P.S. After you write YOUR brilliance, I'd love to read it. I just may include it in my next book! If you're into sharing, send it to jon@jonvroman.com.

PONDER THIS

1. When I graduate, the thing I'll be most proud of that I did during college will be...

   _____

   _____

   _____

   _____

   _____

   _____

2. The one thing that's the most valuable lesson I've taken away from college so far has been...

   _____

   _____

   _____

   _____

   _____

   _____

3. If I were to give one bit of advice to someone just entering college, it would be...

   _____

   _____

   _____

   _____

   _____

   _____

Want to share? Email jon@jonvroman.com.

MEET THE AUTHOR

Jon Vroman is a college speaker, personal coach, ultramarathon runner, proud papa, loving husband, and founder of the Front Row Foundation.

For over two decades now, Jon has had an impact on over 75,000 college students throughout the United States and Canada with his speeches, workshops, and coaching programs.

He is committed to helping students lead themselves and others by becoming more deeply engaged on campus and within their communities.

For more information or to inquire about Jon's speaking schedule, please visit www.FrontRowOnCampus.com.

JON'S FAVORITE QUOTES

Yesterday's over my shoulder,
so I can't look back for too long,
there's just too much to see waiting in front of me,
and I know that I just can't go wrong.

–Jimmy Buffett

Problems are not stop signs, they are guidelines.

–Robert Schuller

Pain is temporary. It may last a minute, or an hour, or a day, or a year, but eventually it will subside and something else will take its place. If I quit, however, it lasts forever.

–Lance Armstrong

Seek not to learn, but to think. Seek not to accept what is told you, but to question. It is a good student who will question what is taught him and it is a good professor who, if he is not sure of his ground, will link arms with the student and say, "let us go and find out." Remember that fifteen units of study a semester may eventually lead to a degree but not necessarily to a real education. You will find that the mind is not a pail to fill, but a dynamo to start working.

–From a speech by a university president to a gathering of students

JON SAYS...

When your *why* has heart, your *how* gets legs.

The best questions to ask others are the ones they want answers to.

You cannot not matter.

There are no failures in life, just moments of discovery.

Be the person you wish to meet in others.

NOTES

NOTES

NOTES

WHEN WOULD NOW BE A GOOD TIME TO START LIVING COLLEGE LIFE IN THE FRONT ROW?

WWW.FRONTROWONCAMPUS.COM

\ 0 /

Made in the USA
Charleston, SC
20 June 2011